I AM A GOOD DIGITAL CITIZEN

I AM
STRONG
ONLINE

RACHAEL MORLOCK

PowerKiDS
press™

NEW YORK

Published in 2020 by The Rosen Publishing Group, Inc.
29 East 21st Street, New York, NY 10010

First Edition

Editor: Elizabeth Krajnik
Book Design: Reann Nye

Photo Credits: Cover antoniodiaz/Shutterstock.com; p. 5 Syda Productions/Shutterstock.com; p. 7 ESB Professional/Shutterstock.com; p. 9 mangpor2004/Shutterstock.com; p. 11 Valeriy_G/iStock/Getty Images Plus/Getty Images; p. 13 vectorfusionart/Shutterstock.com; p. 15 Hero Images/Getty Images; p. 17 Monkey Business Images/Shutterstock.com; p. 19 Bloomicon/Shutterstock.com; p. 21 Michael Candelori/Shutterstock.com; p. 22 GagliardiImages/Shutterstock.com.

Cataloging-in-Publication Data
Names: Morlock, Rachael.
Title: I am strong online / Rachael Morlock.
Description: New York : PowerKids Press, 2020. | Series: I am a good digital citizen | Includes glossary and index.
Identifiers: ISBN 9781538349724 (pbk.) | ISBN 9781538349748 (library bound) | ISBN 9781538349731 (6pack)
Subjects: LCSH: Internet and children–Juvenile literature. | Internet–Safety measures–Juvenile literature. | Privacy, Right of–Juvenile literature.
Classification: LCC HQ784.I58 M673 2020 | DDC 004.67'80289–dc23

Manufactured in the United States of America

CPSIA Compliance Information: Batch #CSPK19. For Further Information contact Rosen Publishing, New York, New York at 1-800-237-9932.

CONTENTS

BE YOUR BEST ONLINE 4

STRONG AND SECURE 6

WHAT'S A PASSWORD? 8

WEAK PASSWORDS 10

STRONG PASSWORDS. 12

PASSWORDS ARE PRIVATE 14

SECURITY. 16

OUTSMARTING HACKERS 18

STRONG SETTINGS 20

YOUR DIGITAL FOOTPRINT . . . 22

GLOSSARY 23

INDEX 24

WEBSITES 24

BE YOUR BEST ONLINE

Many kinds of people use the Internet for many kinds of reasons. But they all have one thing in common—they're all digital citizens! If you use the Internet, then you're a digital citizen, too. Being a good digital citizen is about being your best online. That means being fair, respectful, and safe.

5

STRONG AND SECURE

Every digital citizen has a digital footprint, or a record of how they act online. Your footprint is tied to your online **profiles** and activities. You wouldn't want someone else using your profiles or personal **information**! Good digital citizens take charge by being strong and secure, or safe from danger or harm, online.

7

WHAT'S A PASSWORD?

A password is like a secret handshake. If you know the handshake, you can unlock a digital **device**, log on to a computer, or sign in to an online profile. Creating strong passwords keeps you and your personal information safe. Following basic guidelines can help you make strong passwords.

WEAK PASSWORDS

A weak password is one that a friend or even a stranger could easily guess. Weak passwords are simple. Some use just one word with no capital letters or numbers. Passwords are also weak if they use your nickname, the name of your pet, or personal information such as your birthday.

STRONG PASSWORDS

You should try to make your passwords complex, or not simple. Most passwords need to be at least eight **characters** long. A strong password is made up of a mix of numbers, **symbols**, and uppercase and lowercase letters. Passwords should be hard for others to guess but easy for you to remember.

13

PASSWORDS ARE PRIVATE

Keeping your passwords private, or secret, is one of the best ways to keep yourself safe online. Besides your parents or other trusted adults, no one else should know your passwords—not even your friends! It's important to use different passwords for different profiles. You should change your passwords often to keep them strong and secure.

SECURITY

It's also important to keep digital devices strong. Security is about making sure your phones, tablets, computers, and **software** are safe. You can keep your devices secure by being careful about what you do online. Think twice or ask an adult before clicking on a link or **downloading** anything!

OUTSMARTING HACKERS

When you're online, you might see offers of free music, games, or apps. Sometimes, free downloads have **viruses**. Hackers are people who use your computer or information without asking, often through viruses. You can outsmart hackers by keeping your passwords strong and your devices secure.

19

STRONG SETTINGS

Hackers can also use the information you share online. Another way to protect yourself is to use strong privacy settings. These settings control who sees what you share online. With the help of an adult, you can decide what settings are best for you. Privacy settings keep your personal information safe.

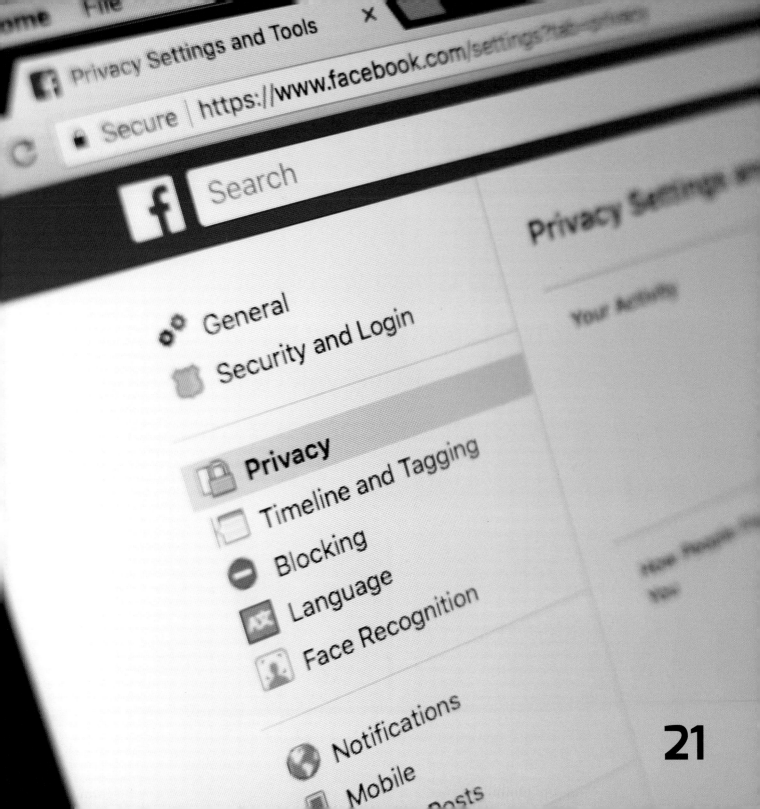

Privacy Settings and Tools

Privacy Settings a

X

https://www.facebook.com/settings?tab=priv

Secure | https://www.facebook

Search

Privacy Settings

Your Activity

General

Security and Login

Privacy

Timeline and Tagging

Blocking

Language

Face Recognition

Notifications

Mobile

21

YOUR DIGITAL FOOTPRINT

You can keep your devices, profiles, and information safe when you're online. Strong passwords and privacy settings and careful Internet use will help you stay safe. Good digital citizens take charge of their own security and privacy. When you're strong online, it's easier to have a good digital footprint!

GLOSSARY

character: A letter, mark, number, sign, or symbol used in writing or printing.

device: A tool used for a certain purpose.

download: To copy information from one computer to another, often over the Internet.

information: Knowledge or facts about something.

profile: Information about someone on a certain computer, website, or app.

software: Programs that run on computers and perform certain tasks.

symbol: Something that stands for something else.

virus: A usually hidden computer program that causes harm.

INDEX

A
activities, 6
adults, 14, 16, 20

C
characters, 12
computers, 8, 16, 18

D
danger, 6
devices, 8, 16, 18, 22
digital footprint, 6, 22
downloads, 18

F
friends, 10, 14

G
guidelines, 8

H
hackers, 18, 20

I
Internet, 4, 22

L
link, 16

P
passwords, 8, 10, 12, 14, 18, 22
personal information, 6, 8, 10, 20
phones, 16
privacy settings, 20, 22
profiles, 6, 8, 14, 22

S
security, 16, 22
software, 16
stranger, 10

T
tablets, 16

V
viruses, 18

WEBSITES

Due to the changing nature of Internet links, PowerKids Press has developed an online list of websites related to the subject of this book. This site is updated regularly. Please use this link to access the list: www.powerkidslinks.com/digcit/strong